Leaving the Pigeonhole

Please follow at: http://leavingthepigeonhole.blogspot.com/

Leaving the Pigeonhole

A Personal Revolution

Valeria Berumen

ISBN 978-0-557-32377-7

This book is dedicated to the countless number of individuals that have wasted endless hours on tedious, mundane, unnecessary busy work confined to a small cubicle in hopes that their tireless compliance will open opportunities of growth in their careers; and to the managers who have emphatically responded to such efforts with:

"You can't do it", "It's not going to happen" and "That's impossible".

To them I contest, ***JUST YOU WAIT AND SEE!***

Acknowledgments

First I would like to thank Michelle Knox for her countless contributions to the book: the hours of editing, the research and help with the text. Moreover, I would like to thank Michelle for her invaluable friendship and support.

I must thank my friend and former professor Peter Antoniou, MIBA, DBA, whose lectures served as the catalyst for this project. Peter is one of those great professors that make the impossible seem possible. Kudos!

I would like to thank my mother, Bertha for her boundless support on this project as well as those that have preceded it and those to follow.

With my deepest gratitude and most sincere love, I thank my daughters Maya and Mia for their unwavering belief that their mother is capable of achieving anything she sets forth to achieve. Their untainted view of life inspires me beyond words.

Finally, I would like to honor my father Catarino Berumen, who I miss dearly and whose unconditional love and words have inspired me throughout my life. I can only imagine my father's eyes filled with pride and joy at the manifestation of my work. I love you dearly now and forever…

Table of Contents

Preface

I began writing this book after having spent the last four years of my life working for an organization that treated me like a third class citizen; meanwhile I was pursuing a degree in Business Administration. I would often justify my situation by telling myself that the organization's caste system was based on one's level of education and expertise and that as soon as I earned my degree I would be able to move up in the organization. I couldn't have been more wrong. During those four years I performed my job duties to the best of my ability and I was doing a darn good job at it too.

Finally when I completed my degree it seemed that my conditions only worsened as I had apparently become a threat to a couple of individuals higher up on the chain of command. For the next six months I was put through a series of demoralizing ordeals that ranged from defamation to discrimination and harassment. For support I turned to a few of my friends and to my surprise most had undergone a similar situation at one point during their careers. Apparently, being pigeonholed was a pretty common phenomenon in which many young upwardly mobile individuals get trapped.

I considered my possibilities, which seemed limited at the time. One was to leave the organization and pursue of a new career, however, that was out of the question as we were in the middle of the financial crisis and with unemployment at an all time high it wasn't feasible or wise to leave. Another option was to lay low in my position until the financial crisis improved and there were more jobs on the market. My final option was to force the organization to see me and to recognize me for whom and what I was; a true professional.

Years ago during a venting session a friend once told me "Don't ever let anyone hold your mirror". Meaning that I was the only one that could dictate who and what I am and with that in mind I opted for the latter. I stayed in the organization and began a lawsuit against the organization on the basis of discrimination and harassment. During my four years at the organization, while they had given me a lot they had taken even more, but the one thing I was determined that they would not take away from me was my dignity. And so, my mission of leaving the pigeonhole began. The entire thing resulted in a long dragged out struggle for the organization, they attempted to discredit me about everyone of my allegations, however, in the end the truth prevailed and I was able to not only win my case against the organization but to gain the respect of my peers and my superiors for standing up for myself. Now I am not suggesting that everyone needs to sue the company they work for in order to get some recognition but I am suggesting that anyone that wants to change their life must stand up for what they believe in.

- If you are someone that wants to change the way that people perceive you.
  You may want to read this book.

- If you not only want to change the way that people perceive you but actually want to undergo a personal revolution.
  You may want to read this book.

- If you find yourself often pondering the question "What does that guy have that I don't have?"
  You may want to read this book.

- If you've ever wondered what separates the winners from the losers.
  You may want to read this book.

- If you think that fate has something to do with the "privileged" and the "unprivileged".
  You may want to read this book.

- If you work for someone that treats you badly and often wonder "Why does this always happen to me?"
  You may want to read this book.

- If you are an employer that wants better workers, the kind that grow into great leaders and that remain loyal to you and to your organization.
  You also may want to read this book.

Introduction

Leaving the Pigeonhole explores the underline reasons of why we perpetually create the same reality for ourselves. *Leaving the Pigeonhole* looks at the factors that lead us to building the same types of relationships and landing the same jobs over and over again. It is amazing to think that we have unlimited possibilities and that we may never tap into them, by always sticking to the same familiar roles. In fact, many of us go through life unaware of our potential because we lack the ability to think outside the box and because we become conditioned to the way things are. We begin to believe that we do not have control over the things that happen to us in our lives and that we are not powerful enough to change our conditions; as we move forward in the book you will discover that being powerless is an absolute lie.

The single most important thing that readers can take away from this book is that no one will ever respect you unless you respect yourself first. Self respect alone is the factor that separates the self-made man or woman from the average Joe. There is no magic to it; there are no secrets about it and predestination is a complete myth. Success yields from the actions that we take and the habits that we build; it is not based on luck. There are no quick fixes to becoming a person of character, as character building takes time, effort and experience. Our goal is to offer our readers the tools needed for achieving a sustainable, lasting transformation; one that will enable them not only to see themselves and the world differently but one that will lead to a personal revolution. Unlike most contemporary transformations and makeovers that are designed to cover up our flaws from the outside- in, a personal revolution is a complete transformation that begins from deep within us and grows outwardly and allows us to live our best lives. A personal revolution is about becoming authentic. It all begins in our thoughts and extends to all aspects our lives.

Leaving the Pigeonhole is a short book aimed at those individuals that are seeking a personal revolution, it is aimed at those individuals that are sick and tired of dead end jobs, it is aimed at those individuals that are willing to take the responsibility to building a better future for themselves and those around them. Since you have selected this book from the thousands of change management books that are out there, you are likely the kind of person that wants to grow from the place where you are now. You are likely a self-driven individual with specific career goals in mind, and there is a strong possibility that you are not happy in the position where you are now. Perhaps you are underemployed or working for an organization that is altogether wrong for you.

So what's a guy or gal to do? Our objective is to identify the pigeonholes in which people get stuck and to provide you with the steps to escaping these pigeonholes. *Leaving the Pigeonhole* is designed to arm you with the strategies needed to make a meaningful transformation in your life.

Consequently, *Leaving the Pigeonhole* is divided into three parts. Part one, "The Way Things Are", which explores the five most common workplace pigeonholes. Dissecting these categories and the character traits that complement them will help us to become aware of our individual inherent traits. This will help us to identify the pigeonhole in which we have been casted and the reasons why. Each category has particular character traits that are deeply embedded in an individual's personality and you may have strong traits of one or several of the pigeonhole characteristics.

Part two "The Way Things Can Be; Present and Future", entails the steps of undergoing a personal revolution and provides you readers the tools needed for a successful transformation. In this section we apply the Overbite Change Model to a personal revolution.

The final part; part three is on "Realization for Life", for most people the ultimate goal is to reach a level of self realization with which we are content. That's what we all dream of and the reason that we pursue our dreams. We all want to experience a personal revolution that will allows to become our ideal selves and to live authentically. *Leaving the Pigeonhole* is a prescription to success; all you have to do in order to achieve your goals is apply the steps. However, *Leaving the Pigeonhole,* like any prescribed medication will only yield success if you actually take the steps needed to improve your current condition. No medication will ever work unless you take it.

In part one we look at each of the following pigeonhole types to figure out which most resembles your personality. Then in part two we will walk through the steps needed to break these molds. Here is a brief description of the top 5 workplace pigeonholes:

- **The Yes Man** is the person that we all love to hate. This is a person in a position of servitude who acts in his or her own self-interest by attempting to win the favor of influential people. This person will execute their plans at any cost including the loss of self-respect.

- **The Airhead** is a character that is primarily seen as incompetent and/or stupid. This person is often the victim of office jokes and is easily made the scapegoat.
- **The Know It All** is the annoying person that believes themselves to be right about everything. This person uses his or her intellectual superiority to make himself look good by making others look bad.
- **The Bad Apple** is that individual that has something negative to say about every situation. This person causes the same damage to a department that one bad apple causes a bushel of good ones; this person infects everyone around them with his or her negative attitude.
- **The Slacker** works very hard at not working. We've all encountered the person that uses every excuse in the book in order to avoid doing his or her work.

We encourage you to examine each type with an open mind and to genuinely compare your past and current behaviors with those of the prototypes. This will help you perceive yourselves in a way that others do. This will also help in the subsequent stages of the change management cycle.

Part I

The Way Things Are; Past & Present

Chapter 1

The Pigeonhole

"9 to 5, for service and devotion, you would think that I would deserve a fair promotion. Want to move ahead, but the boss won't seem to let me. I swear sometimes that man is out to get me"... Dolly Parton, 9 to 5 lyrics

Before we explore the individual roles in which people get cast it is important to explore the concept of the pigeonhole. What exactly is a pigeonhole? When did it begin? And, how did the concept make its way into the operation of contemporary business?

Though the use of messenger pigeons dates back to the mid-ages, the concept of pigeonholes in a business setting started in the mid 1800's when Paul Reuter, the founder of Reuter's press agency started using messenger pigeons to deliver news and stock prices back and four between correspondents. The article *Reuter's from pigeons to multimedia players* describes how Reuter started with a fleet of 45 messenger pigeons. The way it worked was by training pigeons to fly back and forth on routine routes without ever straying from such routes. If you are thinking by now, wow, those must have been some smart chickadees to remember all those routes. Well, that is not really the case because the idea was to keep things simple and constant, making the pigeons part of constant rally race, so essentially they do not have to remember anything. All they had to do was to follow the leader; as one pigeon would serve as guide for the next in the series.

The design was very simple; pigeon drawers would be established at each end of a particular route. These drawers were made up of exactly 9 cubicles with and total of 20 pigeons would be assigned to any give route. This breakdown would ensure that there would always be at least one pigeon in flight in either direction. As soon as one pigeon landed in a pigeonhole another would be forced out to fly. Pretty simple, right? Its amazing to think that this simple method was one of the primary and most reliable forms of communication for a period of approximately 50 years beginning in 1860 to about the early 1900's when technology gave birth to the telegram. Once the telegram machine became popular it completely replaced the messenger pigeon system.

Now if you think its amazing how business managed to successfully train pigeons to perform the simple task of flying back and forth without deviation by following the leader, you will find even more astonishing the fact that this system of management has been alive and well in Corporate America for approximately 100 years and is still thriving today.

As incredulous as this may seem, most of us have had the experience at one point of being trapped in pigeonhole were we are falsely classified into an oversimplified category, one that dictates our capabilities. The fallacy in this system of management is that no one wins, not the individual who is being categorizes as they are dictated their potential. Likewise the manager or management team which utilizes this management system does not win as they constantly miss out on opportunities to nurture and grow their employees as people become obediently defiant towards them.

The results of pigeonholing are unhappy employees that go to a job that they are dissatisfied with and work under a management team that they do not respect. After a while an employee develops a chip on the shoulder attitude. Although they may be masters at hiding their dissatisfaction and resentment towards management, every now and then it rears its ugly head and when it does, that person is perceived as not being committed to the team or the organization. Pigeonholing negatively affected the entire organization because it leads to employees that work at a minimal of their potential. This means that the organization misses out on all the talent that individuals can contribute to the company. As a result a business may have low performance levels, low employee morale and high levels of turnover, all of which are very costly and damaging to any organization.

In spite of the damage that pigeonholing causes an organization and to all involved there is no clarity on who is to blame when it does happens. We all take part in it and we are all partially to blame when it happens. And yes, this includes those that it has happened to because nothing can be done to us unless we allow it. As difficult as it may be to imagine being held accountable for having a terrible boss; we are partially to blame for the situation because we choose to stay and tolerate the boss's abuse.

People that get categorized into simple roles find ways to cope with their situation; and sometimes they contribute to their personal confinement by acting out and playing the role that they are given. On the other hand, there are those that rebel against the pigeonholes that they are cast into by becoming blatantly defiant by doing the exact opposite of what are expected of them. This type of rebellion often invites an entire new set of problems, which further marginalizes them from the team.

In order to understand why pigeonholing takes place in the workplace we must understand one thing; pigeonholing happens because for many it is a way of dealing with personal fears and insecurities. In a world of growing complexity and rapid spreading globalization, we must take into consideration the diversity and competition of the workplace. We are currently operating in the most competitive market in the history of Corporate America, with the National Unemployment rate at an alarming 11%, the highest it has been since the mid 80's. People come from all walks of life, from any point on the globe and carry with them their personal views of the world. In addition to that, we are facing a generation phenomenon, in which it is the first time in history that four generations are simultaneously in the workplace. As you can imagine there is a wide range of beliefs and expectations from one group to another. Here's a brief overview of the generations and their work characteristics as outlined by The Learning Café:

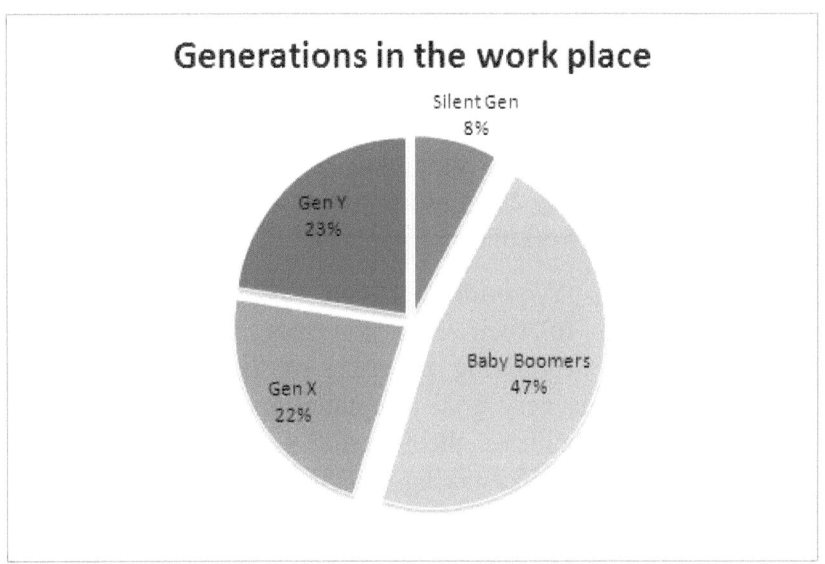

- Silent Generation, born between 1933 and 1945 and make up 8% of the workforce. Generally, individuals from this generation are known to be hard workers, loyal and take care of business before pleasure.
- Baby Boomers, born between 1946 and 1964 and make up 46% of the workforce. This generation is very career orientated with a strong work ethic. This group is generally optimistic and open to change but is notoriously known for being highly competitive. This competitiveness is quite fitting for this generation as they group up during

a time in which the United States was a number one innovator at practically every level; technology, sports, business, education, etc…

- Generation X, born between 1965 and 1976; make up 23% of the workforce. Generation Xers are by far the most independent of all the generations and are often regarded as rebellious by older generations. Conversely, the younger generation perceives them as innovators or pioneers for their generation. Generation Xers seek change within or outside of the system. These individuals work best under minimal supervision and have limited trust towards establishment. Many of the individuals from this generation were latch key kids as both parents where in the workforce. Generation Xers learned to fend for themselves very early in their lives and have carried these skills to the workplace.
- Generation Y, born between 1977 and 1998, are individuals in their 20's to early 30's entering the workforce accounting for 23% of the workforce. This generation is very goal orientated and works within the system to achieve their goals. Generation Y, unlike Generation X, like taking direction from their superiors. Gen Y-ers are oftentimes regarded as having a sense of entitlement. The fact is that for many Gen Y-ers the world has evolved around them for as long as they can remember and they expect no different from the workplace.

Now let's look at how these groups interact in the workplace. Take a look at any IT Department; look around who's occupying the cubicles? Who is sharing the limited space? I am sure you'll find a good mix of Baby Boomers, Gen X-ers and Gen Y-ers and a least one person from every continent.

At first glance, things may look pretty normal and mellow, but each group has its own ideology on how to get things done and their own work ethic. The difference in each group's approach to a job can and often does leads to communication issues, competition, high levels of stress and to an overall decline in moral. This type of workplace leads to high turnover rates which hobbles a department's ability to work efficiently and productively. Imagine that you had ESP and that you could hear the thoughts of those working in a typical IT department; you might hear something like this.

> **Gen Y, thinks:** "Gen X-ers are a bunch of whiners that do nothing but complain about the workplace but don't do anything about it."
>
> **Gen X-ers, thinks:** "Gen Y-ers are arrogant, entitled little snobs. Crybabies!"
>
> **Gen Y and Gen X think:** "That Baby Boomers are self-absorbed, workaholic, maniacs! Those guys should seek mental health and get a life."
>
> **Gen X and the Baby Bombers think about the Silent Generation:** "Are they still here, man! He/she should really go home and rest."
>
> **Gen Y thinks about Silent Generation:** "They're so cute!"
>
> **The Silent Generation thinks about the whole bunch:** "Nothing ever changes!"

So who's right? Well, they all are. Everyone is partially right because every story has more than one truth to it. Each group sees things differently based on their experience, point of view and cultural norms. In fact, each individual perceives things slightly different than another based on their personal experience. This concept is linked to Albert Einstein's the law of relativity. The law of relativity state that there can be several truths to one event depending on the relativity and perspective of the observer to that event. One person can perceive a behavior one way and be right, while another perceives the same behavior and has a completely different opinion and can also be right. Here is Albert Einstein's theory:

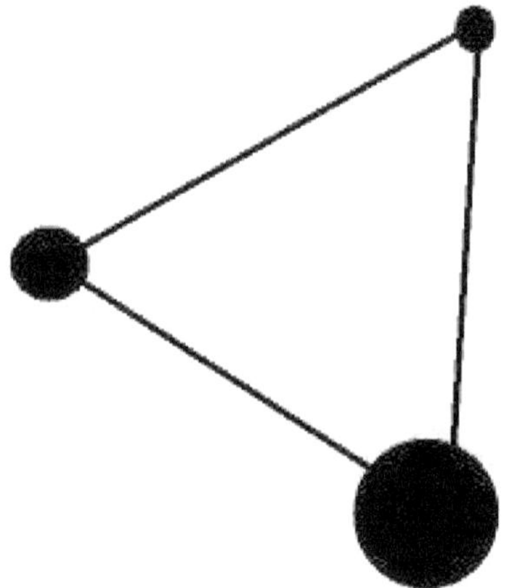

Relativity of simultaneity: *Two events, simultaneous for some observer, may not be simultaneous for another observer if the observers are in relative motion.*

However, the real root of pigeonholing is based in fear. In the office it often starts with two dimensional people. We live and operate in a multi-dimensional world, where possibilities and people's potentials are limitless, yet there are individuals who fail to see the world from a holistic perspective therefore they fail to see the potential benefit that individuals have to offer an organization beyond the simple role that they are casts into. These individuals use pigeonholing as a coping mechanism, as it is highly impossible for them to see beyond two dimensions. They perceive an individual only for what he or she is now and they crystallize them expecting that person stay to there forever, which is a very unrealistic view on life as change is inevitable. Moreover, two dimensional people lack the ability to think of a person's potential; they lack the ability to see that people can be an organization's most valuable asset. Think for a moment about the elements that make up an organization. Let's use a 5 star hotel as an example: Suppose you have paid for a vacation at a 5 star luxury hotel. Once you arrived you find a beauty property with elegant decorations. So far so good, right?

But later as you approached the front desk you encountered a very nervous front desk attendant who mixes up your reservation. However, what you don't know is that this person may have been so afraid of his or her manager that they couldn't get their mind clear even to complete your reservation. From that point on your entire trip takes a nose dive. You begin to see patterns in unhappy employees that want nothing more than to put in their 8 hours of work so they can go home. So, regardless of how beautiful the hotel maybe it is only a shell where business is conducted and the people that work there are the primary factor that determines the hotels rank.

Two dimensional individuals believe that there is only the "us" and the "them". They never consider that the "us" and the "them" are one and that everyone in an organization is on the same team. A two dimensional person would immediately accuse the front desk clerk of ruining everything, failing to see that perhaps that person's room was changed due to a plumbing situation or that another family with the same surname had just arrived the same day or simply that the front desk was understaffed and that the attendant had more responsibility and volume than he could handle.

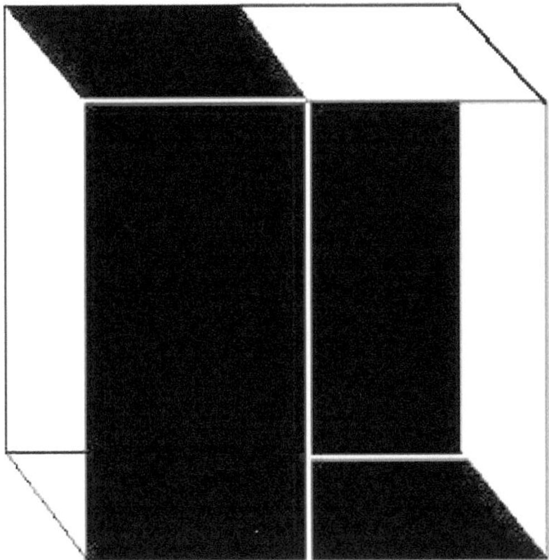

On the other hand someone who is multidimensional can see that it is all a matter of perspective and that things are not always as they appear to be. A multidimensional person can look at the same problem from various angles to come up with the best and most logical solution. A multidimensional person knows that the only way that a 5 star hotel can deliver excellence is if everyone on the team is working together to make the customer's experience as pleasant as possible.

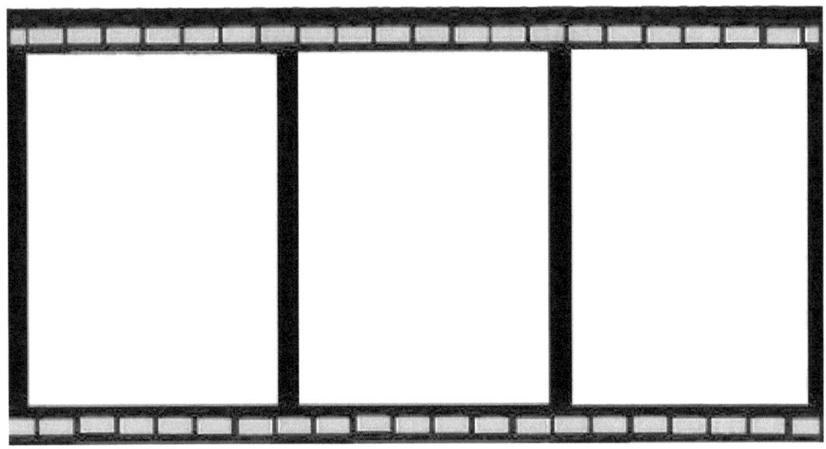

Chapter 2

The Roles

"Theater is, of course, a reflection of life.

Maybe we have to improve life before we can hope to improve theater." W.R. Inge

Now that we have covered the origin of the pigeonhole and the impact that it has on contemporary business let's dive into the top five workplace pigeonholes. To accurately describe each of the pigeonholes, I've compiled a typecast for each character based on my personal observation of the workplace. During my career, I have, as many of us, experienced a number of firsthand accounts of pigeonholing. I also have had the misfortune of landing in a few of those roles myself. Like many working adults, I began pursuing a bachelor's degree in my late twenties; I was managing school while working an entry-level position, in hopes of graduating and moving up in the organization. Unfortunately, four years later when I received my degree in Business Administration; I found that few people in the organization could not see beyond my role of an Administrative Assistant where I had started. This experience was very frustrating.

The roles in which I have been trapped have ranged from the "Know It All" to the "Airhead" and a few others over the years that I have been in the work force. For several years I played the role of a "Cinderella" which is a role of the being perfect assistant. I always expected that my dedication would be interpreted as loyalty and desire to grow, but I was always misunderstood as being foolish and people took advantage of me. Putting up with years of abuse took a toll on my health, and my health declined severely. I later developed a very painful stress related condition called TMJ. The TMJ caused me chronic pain and worst yet, unknowing to me it began affecting my psychological state. Over of few short years I developed terrible dyslexia like symptoms stemming from stress all the while I was unaware of what was going on with me. The entire ordeal cost me royally as at work and in other aspects of my life. My boss chalked up my declining performance to me simply being stupid. At the same time I had began a pursuing a Master's degree in Business Administration, again my ignorance about my condition and lack of treatment forced me to have to leave the program as my performance there too began to decline, my colleagues and professors lost faith in me and thought I was completely unqualified to be in the program. After exchanging a few personal experiences with friends I found that many of my friends had had similar experiences of being pigeonholed, so I started collecting the information for this book. We'll look at the steps on undergoing a personal revolution in Part II but now let's start by looking at the specific roles that people get cast into.

As you read the upcoming sections keep in mind that you may identify with one or several of the roles described, this is completely normal and expected as we are malleable and constantly changing. We also demonstrate different roles when we are in different circumstances. However, it will be helpful to try to identify with one or two dominant roles as this will assist you with a developing a transformation plan of action and road map for your personal revolution.

Each pigeonhole type has two major elements which must be analyzed and understood before any changes can be made: the first element is **"YOU"**. First and foremost you must understand the pigeonhole that you have been trapped in. Secondly you must understand the environment and those around you in order to make the appropriate changes. Both sides are equally important; if you strategize without paying attention to the factors that contribute to your current condition, your attempts at transformation will seem false. If you go forward without paying attention to those around you, you will make terrible mistakes and limit your potential.

Dr. Deepak Chopra explains in The Spontaneous Fulfillment of desire; harnessing the infinite power or coincidence (2003), that understanding human relationships is one of the most important keys to success. In the workplace we tend to think that our relationships exist separately from our true thoughts and feelings. We may acknowledge that we need to be cordial and nice in order to get along but it is the ability to create positive human relationships beyond simply getting along that creates true networks and synchronicity in the work place. Synchronicity is a concept in which a team works so well that they are more powerful than they would be independently. For instance 4 men rowing a boat and creating the force of 6 men rowing together, but each rowing independently would only create the force of one man rowing. Here is an exercise that will help you understand the messages and signals that take place in your workplace.

Pretend you are watching a silent movie of your own life.

What do you see?

What you see on the screen is what other people see as well and that's how people perceive you. The people around you can only observe your actions not your thoughts and intentions. People cannot get in your head and read your inner thoughts, struggles and frustrations, they only see as far as the eye allows.

Now pretend that are watching a movie with sound, but no picture.

WHAT DO YOU HEAR?

Well what you hear is what others hear as well and those are the messages that you send out. It is important to understand both how people perceive your actions and the messages that you send out in order to understand why you have been cast into a particular pigeonhole.

The second element to a personal revolution involves understanding those around you. Pay attention to people that you admire and/or respect, the company cultural and its value system. Setting yourself aside is really about getting yourself in tune with what people like, want and expect. This helps us map out a strategy for change. Here is one final exercise that will help you understand your environment.

Pretend that you are a camera guy making a movie about your company.

WHAT DO SEE?

What you see from behind the lens can be considered the company's culture. Is it chaotic or organized and efficient? Notice how people behave towards each other; those are the company norms. Are people courteous and respectful towards each other or are they rude and disrespectful? Whatever your company norms may be, keep in mind that one's environment is a mirror reflection of the inner characters of individual employees, including your own. Generally, if an individual finds other people unfriendly it is often because he or she provokes that reaction.

If our environment truly mirrors our lives and it appears that everything about our environment is flawed, then it's it our responsibility to stop blaming others and to begin to take responsibility for our own lives? *Leaving the Pigeonhole* will teach you that you are the architect of you existence and that your surroundings reflect precisely what you have built. Likewise, *Leaving the Pigeonhole* entails the steps needed to take responsibility and empowers the reader to effect change.

Now that you have contemplated your past actions, the messages that you send out and the company norms, let's begin to explore each of the pigeonhole types. Remember to keep an open mind and to be honest with yourself about the pigeonholes that you identify with.

Pigeon Profile

Industry: You will find one in any industry.

Sex: Male or Female

Career stage: Across all career stages.

Lifestyle: Enjoys living a lavish life and tends to possess quality material objects, nice house, car, etc.

Employment history: In middle management or aspiring to become part of the management team.

Psychological characteristics: This person is about winning and getting what they want. They will do whatever it takes to accomplish their goals.

Beliefs & values: Believes that winning is more important than self-respect and values material rewards far more than people.

Motives: Money, power and self serving greed.

Who's that Pigeon?

The Yes Man

"The dog is a yes-animal. Very popular with

people who can't afford a yes man." Robertson Davies

The Yes Man is the guy or gal that we all love to hate. This is the person that goes around smiling and nodding their head at everything the boss has to say. It doesn't matter if the boss is right or wrong; a Yes Man/Woman gives their full and unquestionable obedience to his or her employer in hopes of building a pristine reputation with them as well as with other influential people in the organization in order to manipulate them in his or her favor. This person jumps through hoops, fetches and jumps at every whim that the boss can conceive of. Yes Men and Women are often successful with these tactics because having a flunky around feeds every vein man's ego. Egotistical people like having these types of people around in order to feel important. However, the tactic is not entirely fool proof and can easily backfire, making the Yes Man/Woman look like a blatant manipulator.

Contrary to the relationships that Yes Men and Women have with their employers, they typically have poor relationships with their peers and subordinates, the reason being is that the Yes Man/Woman is instrumental in the type casting and pigeonholing of others. Employers tend to use them as examples for others and of course, the Yes Man/Woman loves it. They often fuel the attention by whispering bugs into an employer's ear about their peers. However, becoming a Yes Man does not guarantee a person's success or longevity in an organization because people usually want them out and often times conspire against them in hopes of uncovering them for the phonies that they are.

Becoming a Yes Man is a trap in and of itself because life is not absolute. No one person can always be right and that includes the boss; he or she knows it and so should you. An employer hires an individual because they expect that person to have a particular skill set and a certain level of accountability. However, Yes Men/Women tend to be seen as puppets of their superiors with no integrity or free will. These relationships are entirely unhealthy and not beneficial to anyone. A relationship between an employee and his or her superior should be one of checks and balances in both directions. That's why an employer hires experts in particular fields. Employers expect the person they've hired is an expert in their field and that they understand the job better than anyone else including them, that's why they have been selected.

Don't get me wrong; there are many perks to always going along with the boss, for instance being viewed as a favorite; another benefit is being considered one of the team and often being asked to participate in lunch meetings with your superiors. The Yes Man/Woman's obedience and loyalty tends to earns them favors or perks, for instance enjoying a higher level of liberty that none of the co-workers are allowed. When things go well for the boss, the workplace can be a utopia for the Yes Man. His/her boss continuously meets his goals and the Yes Man/Woman is a part of making it happen. Naturally the Yes Man looks good. These situations can earn the Yes Man garner accolades and positive reinforcement. This all sounds great, right? And it is great while things go well for the boss everything is rosy peachy; everybody is happy, however, the trouble begins when things start to go wrong.

The minute that things turn out wrong the Yes Man becomes the scapegoat in order for the boss to save face. Sometimes unfairly blamed and other times the responsibility is completely justified. Why? Well, because the Yes Man has failed to fulfill his duties to serve as a "check and balance" to the boss's actions. Furthermore his unquestionable obedience has contributed to the boss's demise. If you just go around doing whatever is asked of you simply because your boss made a request, then you are part of the problem.

This is how it works. We all operate in a sequential world, which includes business: If I do this then my competitors will do that. If I raise or lower my prices, then my customers will either go elsewhere with their business or patronize my company more frequently. These sequences are followed in every realm of life, sometimes with visible and direct outcomes and sometimes with long term effects that only become noticeable after an extended period of time. These types of sequences snowball into occurring, this is something like the "Butterfly Effect"; the idea is that something as minor as a butterfly flapping its wings in Brazil can become the catalyst that sets of a series of events that have the potential to snowball and result in a tornado in Texas. Little things can add up or lead down paths which can become huge monstrosities.

Unquestionable obedience is a sure recipe for the demise of any business whether in finance, health care, entertainment or whatever the case may be because the long term affects of these actions can have serious negative repercussions. Looking the other way or going around blindly following a leader simply because he or she is your superior is an irresponsible stand and usually results negatively for all involved.

Downfalls of the Yes Man/Woman:

Though there are many perks to becoming a Yes/Man there are an equal number of pitfalls. The most damaging of all is the decline of self-respect. There is nothing more disheartening and depowering than losing faith in one self. Ordinary people that accomplish magnificent, extra ordinary things in this world are those that carry with them a sure confidence that no matter how bad a situation may become or how unfortunate life may be towards them, they will rise above all opposition and will be victorious.

In a very short period of time Yes Men/Women begin to have doubts about their personal ability to overcome adversity and begin to believe that the only way they will ever get anywhere is through the alliances that they make. This can become a difficult cycle to escape. Outlined below are a few of the pitfalls that Yes Men/Women tend to get trapped in.

- Your reputation is at stake; people lose respect of you.
- Employers cast you into a category of one that is not to be taken seriously.
- People will believe your flattery is false and will lose trust in you.
- You become a scapegoat for anything that goes wrong for your employer.
- You lose your self-respect.

The Yes Man/Women Mind Set
Before and After a Personal Revolution

Before	After
1. Approaches life and their career from a fear-based stand point.	**1. Approaches life from a logical stand point.**
2. Wins favors by offering, flattery and unquestionable obedience.	**2. Wins respect by acting responsibly and earning merits for their efforts.**
3. Uses others for personal benefit.	**3. Is pragmatic and work with others for mutual benefit.**
4. Is not part of the team.	**4. Understands that without a team he or she is nothing.**
5. Makes others look bad in order to make himself look good.	**5. Encourages others to achieve their full potential.**

Pigeon Profile

Industry: Clerical, customer service orientated & hospitality.

Sex: This profile is most typically associated with women, however it is not exclusive to women.

Career stage: Early stages of a career. However this pigeonhole type can haunt someone through their entire career.

Lifestyle: Enjoys living a simple life free of worries.

Employment history: Entry level, clerical or retail.

Psychological characteristics: Their motto is "Don't Worry Be Happy!"

Beliefs & values: They believe that "life is like a box of chocolates you never know what you're gonna get" and nothing could concern them less.

Motives: To have as few responsibilities as possible. Peace of mind is far more important than money.

Who's that Pigeon?

The Airhead

> *"Do something really wrong the first time and no one will ever think to ask you again"... Stewart Gary*

Airheads are usually perceived to be incompetent, dense or just plain stupid. These individuals are often regarded as flighty and are never taken seriously. The airhead pigeonhole manifests itself in two ways: those that use the scatterbrained persona as a strategy and those that have been unable to escape the label of airheads based upon real or imagined incompetence. So let's say there are those that want to be airheads and those that do not want to be airheads.

Although it may seem that no one would ever willingly want to be seen as an airhead there are those that make a career out of playing the airhead role. They do so because being an airhead absolves them from any kind of responsibility. A few years ago I worked for someone that was the perfect example of the deliberate airhead; she made a career out of playing dumb. Once when we were discussing the company's culture and levels of responsibilities, she told me "I'm really good at playing dumb to get what I want". In a strange, pathetic way she was actually proud of the fact that she could deceive people into believing that she was an idiot and to fool them into feeling sorry for her. She further shared that if she acted like she didn't know how to run a particular report or how to fix a particular problem then someone else would step up and fix the problem for her. As a young professional it was really disheartening for me to hear this coming from a woman that was my superior and whom I was expected to respect.

From that point on my perception of this person was changed forever, for obvious reasons I could never consider this person to be a mentor. I believed that this person had no self respect as it was more important for her to have an easy job with minimal responsibilities. Common sense says that a person like this could not and should not be in a position of leadership. However sometimes they are. My ex-supervisor was a manager for to a small department that had a heavy responsibility and her staff resented her for the demands required for the team to be successful. However, the problem was not entirely hers but rather it was an organizational problem because the organizational allowed and fostered this kind of pseudo leadership. The company was the puppeteer that held the strings and she was the perfect puppet. In reality it was the organization that did not realize the importance of a strong work ethic and necessity of good morale for a productive workplace. The company just wanted someone they could maneuver and that is what they had. The downside of her incompetence and the organization's irresponsibility was that the entire staff paid the consequences. When something would go wrong and the staff needed a real leader to turn to for guidance this supervisor did not know what to do. Under extreme circumstances she often broke down in tears, which only added to the already desperate situation.

> *Imagine if you are a staff member in a call center and you have a screaming customer on the phone; you then turn to your supervisor for assistance and she breaks down in tears. Now you not only have a screaming customer to pacify you also have a crying over emotional supervisor to consul.*

Since no one in the organization took her serious it seemed the perception was transferred onto the entire crew. This slacker of a manager set the tone for the department and made it very difficult for someone who desired to advance within the company. Since she felt threatened by hardworking ambitious people she somehow always managed to find a way to sabotage them.

The flipside to the deliberate airhead is the person that is not a true airhead but is categorized into that role by those around them including their peers and their superiors. Being categorized as an airhead can be one of the most frustrating and demoralizing situations because being misunderstood can inhibit your self-confidence. Definitely being made to feel and appearing to be inadequate or incompetent can be despairing to anyone's ego, further extremely damaging to one's career.

The airhead role is one of the most self fulfilling roles anyone can be categorized into because things always go wrong, there is absolutely no doubt about it, and when something does go wrong the airhead automatically becomes the scapegoat for the entire group. The airhead becomes the fall guy for everyone else's incompetency as people rarely own up to their mistakes. So, for that reason an airhead will always self-prophesying. Henry Ford once said "Whether you think that you can, or that you can't, you are usually right."

Typically, a person that is unfairly cast as an airhead does not have the skill set or training needed for the position that they are in or they are simply doing too much. So, again everyone involved has their share of responsibility for this person's deficiencies. I have seen entire departments that count on the one secretary that mixes up meetings, loses documents and can't seem to get quite right. So, how does the management team respond? They give that person more work. It is obvious that individual is has far more work than they can handle, yet the manager or supervisor sets them up for a sure failure rather than taking a step back identifying the root of the problem and helping to correct it by offering help or training or whatever that person may need to accomplish their jobs. What this means for a person who has been cast into the airhead role is that they must work harder than their peers in order to break that mold and to achieve a personal revolution.

Downfalls of becoming an Airhead

The worst thing about being categorized as an airhead is when we begin to believe that we are indeed airheads, believing that that we are powerless to change our situations because we are not smart enough or strong enough to do so. This is a lie that is ingrained in us by those that want to control us, but the reality is that anyone has the power to change their circumstances. Oftentimes those that place others in the category are true airheads themselves and use this pigeonhole as cover up for their own shortcomings.

Another downfall of becoming an airhead is that people believe the airhead to be incompetent and irresponsible. This pigeonhole can truly hamper one's ability to become successful at any given career as people begin to underestimate your capabilities and the airhead is easily made the scapegoat, because they are the weakest link. More often than not others will believe that the airhead is responsible for anything that goes wrong because their credibility quickly diminishes. Outlined below are a few of the pitfalls that the Airhead tends to get trapped in.

- Your peers and your superior lose respect for you.
- Employers do not take you seriously.
- People will believe you are not smart enough to handle a given situation.
- You become the scapegoat for anything that goes wrong.
- You get overlooked when promotion opportunities arise.

The Airhead Mind Set
Before and After a Personal Revolution

Before	After
1. Believes that he/she is not smart enough to manage a given situation.	**1. Believes that he/she is smart enough and strong enough to manage a given situation**
2. Fails to speak up in self defense	**2. Stands up for their rights**
3. Goes with the flow in order to avoid conflicts	**3. Understands that conflict can be necessary sometimes.**
4. Is made the scapegoat for other's mistakes.	**4. Takes responsibility for his or her actions and holds other accountable for theirs.**
5. Does not take himself or his job too seriously.	**5. Holds himself responsible for his job.**

Pigeon Profile

Industry: Any industry most commonly found in white collar jobs.

Sex: Male and Female

Career stage: Across all career stages.

Lifestyle: This person can be a loner and rarely has genuine friends. This person feels that people do not understand him or her.

Employment history: Middle Management or Law Enforcement

Psychological characteristics: This person is all about feeling important, nothing gives them more pleasure than to prove their point.

Beliefs & values: This person is more concerned with "just facts" and feels that facts are important than people's feelings.

Motives: Being Right!

Who's that Pigeon?

The Know It All

"There are three types of people, those that teach,

those that learn and those that think they know it all" Mestre Raiul

Nobody wants to be wrong but no one can always be right. While it feels nice to earn praise and recognition for having a wealth of knowledge and expertise, however being a Know It All can be a double edged sword. Whenever people need your expertise they will come to you for help, but, most of the time peers and superiors will fail to recognize the Know It All for their contributions. If you are an individual that believes that you know it all, then you have created your own pigeonhole. The Know It All is the annoying person that thinks they know everything and that never fails to correct everyone around them. Unfortunately people usually grow resentful of them very quickly.

This character sends out a message that says that they can never grow or become a better person than they are now. If you believe that you know it all, your attitude makes the bold statement that you are perfect and that everyone around you is not. In general people dislike and recent anyone that makes them feel inferior, in fact it only takes one time of humiliating a person for them to lose respect for of you for ever.

People that know it all stand alone as everyone works against them to prove them wrong. Why? Because knowing it all, first of all is impossible and secondly believing that one knows it all negatively sets one apart from the rest of the group. Imagine for a moment that someone could actually know everything there is to know about a particular industry or job; essentially that person would not need anyone, not superiors or subordinate. Knowing everything means that you don't need guidance from your superiors or anyone else for that matter and this comes across as arrogance which only serves to alienate others.

The Know It All similarly to the Yes Man becomes masters at making themselves look good at the expense of making others look incompetent. Their peers tend to work against them and are happy to see them fail. By far the most damaging aspect of being a Know it All is that this person hampers an organizations ability to be productive.

In economics there is the principle of Production Possibility Frontier (PPF) originated by Paul A. Samuelson, Nobel Prize laureate. His concept was that that if there are several countries competing and trading in one market, the optimal situation is to allow each country to focus on producing what they produce best; even if one country is particularly good at producing everything, allowing each country to produce their number one product will yield the best outcomes. This principle can be applied to any workplace as staffs are continuously trading and exchanging information, product and knowledge. The most productive work place are those in which everyone does their own job and where the Know It All allows people to be productive. The Know It All cannot and should not meddle in everyone's business; it is destructive, and will serve only to further alienate the Know It All. You don't have to be a Nobel Prize laureate to know that when people are empowered to do what they do best the outcomes will be amazing.

The Downfalls of Becoming a Know it All are:

In general it seems that the Know It All ends up with a bad reputation because people tend to feel intimated by those that are smarter than they are; particularly if that person goes out of their way to flaunt the fact that they know more than them. As discussed in chapter 1, we are currently operating in a highly competitive world and being a Know It All makes you a target for anyone with dominant short comings to cover up.

Below is a list of the issues that most Know It All's encounter on a daily basis.

- Everyone around you is annoyed by your constant demonstration of intellectual superiority.
- Pointing out other's mistakes cause your peers and your superiors grow to resent you.
- People work against you and they are happy when you fail.
- People higher than you on the chain of command are threatened by you.
- You are typically not considered to be a team player.

The Know it All Mind Set
Before and After a Personal Revolution

1. Constantly seeks approval by superiors.	**1. Give himself and other the credit that they have earned.**
2. Gains approval by making others look bad.	**2. Gains respect by acting responsibly and by helping others to achieve their full potential.**
3. Is intolerant of the mistakes of Others.	**3. Looks as his mistakes before accusing others.**
4. Is not part of the team.	**4. Becomes the most valuable player on a team.**
5. Uses his/her intellectually superiority as a weapon.	**5. Uses his/her intellect as valuable tool to achieve organizational goals.**

Pigeon Profile

Industry: There is one in every industry.

Sex: More often associated with men but women too can fit the type.

Career stage: This type cast sticks with a person throughout their entire career.

Lifestyle: This person to displays an attitude of dissatisfaction towards most things in their lives.

Employment history: As it can be found in any industry it can also be seen in any position.

Psychological characteristics: This person tends to have an extremely negative outlook on life.

Beliefs & values: Believes that live is hard and believes that everyone against him or her.

Motives: Fear and insecurity.

Who's that Pigeon?

The Bad Apple

"For there is nothing either good or bad, but thinking makes it so."... Shakespeare

Most of us could easily point out the Bad Apple in any group. She may be the friend who is always dissatisfied with the food, whatever the restaurant, never hesitating to share her experience with the management. He may be the know-it-all that never fails to correct everyone around him. The difficulty lies in acknowledging when you are the one who is the bad apple. Consequently the biggest obstacle to a bad apple breaking out of the pigeonhole is the realization that they are indeed a bad apple. This individual justifies his behavior by believing they are the only ones who see that the work environment is unbearable. They are not shy about their dismay, not because they want to change things but because they want to be heard. They are unaware or unconcerned that others view this as just complaining. In addition to their words, the bad apples use facial expressions, body language, and a consistently bad attitude hoping to convey his or her dissatisfaction with the company, department, supervisor, and/or position.

Conveniently enough, the bad apple views herself as a victim of his or her circumstances without the responsibility or power to change anything. While the bad apple may be a productive employee, his negativity overshadows that productivity. This bad attitude can covertly affect his colleagues causing morale to plummet or simply force others to avoid working with him or her altogether. The low morale and exclusion feeds the feeling of victimhood in the bad apple, which only reinforces negative behavior and creates a seemingly endless cycle of feeling persecuted. The bad apple doesn't want to lead and refuses to follow, so they become viewed as an obstacle to the organization's objectives. The bad apple's reputation results in missed opportunities for both the employee and the organization and many times they are deemed of little benefit to the organization and in the worst of scenarios end up being terminated.

If you and your employer are not a good fit, you can easily fall into the bad apple trap. You may feel that changing jobs is not an option so you endure this bad relationship because you feel that there is no other alternative.

The Downfalls of Being a Bad Apple are:

As you have read there are practically no benefits to being a bad apple; perhaps the few benefits that a person may find in playing the role of the bad apple are self indulgence and self gratification for rebelling against the management team and/or or organization with whom you are dissatisfied. However, that doesn't change anything for the bad apple or anyone else around them. On the other hand there are countless negative consequences that come from being a bad apple. Below is a list of the types of problems the Bad Apple deals with on a daily basis.

- You are classified as difficult persons and people believe that you are a trouble maker.
- People fear that you are mentally unstable and may snap one day.
- Your constant complaining lowers the morale of everyone around you.
- You are chronically made the scapegoat when things go wrong.

- Your peers and your superiors resent your chronic negativity.
- You are not part of the team and no one looks out for you.

The Bad Apple's Frame of Mind
Before and After a Personal Revolution

1. Has a very pessimistic outlook on life.	**1. Has a logical and reasonable outlook on life and offers solutions when he/she is unhappy with a situation.**
2. Finds a reason to complain about absolutely everything.	**2. Tries to make the best out of a bad situation.**
3. Feels like everyone is out to get him.	**3. Does not take things personally.**
4. Tries to make things as difficult as possible for everyone.	**4. Contributes to a work place that runs smoothly and works productively.**

Pigeon Profile

Industry: You will find one in any industry, more often in entry level position or mid- management.

Sex: More commonly associated with Males. However women can fall into this trap too.

Career stage: Across all career stages because it becomes a habitual lifestyle.

Lifestyle: Enjoys living easy.

Employment history: Not too ambitions, lays low and does as little as possible.

Psychological characteristics: This person finds an excuse to get out of doing their work. They can be master manipulators or simply not care.

Beliefs & values: Believes that lunch is the most important hour of the work day.

Motives: To do a little as possible

Who's that Pigeon?

The Slacker

"I slack; therefore I am... Doing nothing"...Dave White

The slacker is the person that shows up to work and works very had at not working. Slackers have minimal ambitions and see themselves as having many limitations. They never seem to have enough time; they never have enough help or guidance to overcome their shortcomings and everything that goes wrong is always someone else's fault. They feel as if people are always coming to them with issues that are "NOT THEIR PROBLEM". They always find an excuse and a reason to complain about excess work; for some reason they feel like this will buy them some sympathy from everyone around them, when all it does is annoy people. This type of individual puts all their efforts into making up excuses and finding ways to pass the buck onto someone else, and although there are many reasons why these types of people operate the way they do; the main reason why the slacker gets away with the things they do it is because the organization fosters their behavior as part of the company's culture and norms. The only way a slacker can get away with doing practically nothing most of the time, is because the company allows it, whether directly or indirectly. Consider that an organization and its norms are like a fish. A fish changes direction head first, then the body follows, similarly to what happens in an organization; slackers they set the pace of what is expected and acceptable in an organization. For instance if one person is allowed to come in 15 minutes late on a regular basis then their peers will begin to feel they have the same rights and will begin to do the same. If a slacker is allowed to miss deadlines then what's to stop a person that works hard and that is dedicated to their job from doing the same.

Another reason why slackers do the things they do it's because they truly believe themselves to be pigeonholed; in a hole that they have created for themselves and that they can see no escape from. Typically this person is in middle management and has no hope of ever making a leap into true leadership role as a Director or Vice President. These individuals have often times seen the prime of their careers come and go and feel that they don't need to work hard because they are content where they are at.

In the worst of cases there are those Slackers who have founded their entire careers based on a foundation of mediocrity by making "just getting by" their primary goal. They justify their actions by saying "That guy can do it for me" or "What's 10 minutes here or there; I stay here late plenty of nights" unfortunately, their justifications are unfounded and in reality their attitudes and actions do make a great impact on a department's general morale and overall performance. The fact that certain individuals can be excused from responsibilities and get away with it sends out the message that it acceptable for anyone else to do the exact same thing. And they do!

> A typical conversation between a Slacker Manager and his Subordinate would go something like this:
>
> *Staff member come to Slacker Manager and says: "Do you have 2 minutes?"*
>
> *Slacker Manager replies: "I have a meeting." And then runs off.*

Notice how the manager never stops to ask the level of urgency of the staff's matter. The manager doesn't ask to set up another time to discuss the matter after the meeting. They simply dismiss that person officially making it not their problem.

Downfalls of Becoming a Slacker

For the most part Slackers feel as if they have out smarted their superiors, their co-workers and the organization as a whole. However what a Slacker really does by acting irresponsibly and incompetently towards their job responsibilities is create a trap for themselves from which they cannot escape. Their actions limit their possibilities of ever liberating themselves from the place where they are now. This means they can never grow because growing would require that they put in some work and Slackers are not capable of harnessing the will needed, as slacking of is as habit forming as working hard. So giving a Slacker the opportunity to grow would be like offering a person that is completely out of shape the opportunity to run in a marathon. It would be a complete waste of effort.

The Slacker's Frame of Mind
Before and After a Personal Revolution

1. Approaches his/her job responsibilities irresponsibly constantly testing the limitations of what they can get away with.	**1. Approaches his/her job responsibilities proactively.**
2. Uses ever excuse to get out of working.	**2. Works with others to become more productive.**
3. Uses others for personal benefit.	**3. Is pragmatic and work with others for mutual benefit.**

Part II

The Way Things Can Be; Present & Future

Chapter 3

A Personal Revolution

"Love and work are the cornerstones of our humanness"...Sigmund Freud

As you read through this chapter please keep in mind that Rome was not built in a day and likewise it would be impossible for us to undergo a personal revolution in a relatively short period of time. Since a Personal Revolution aims at making a core change it is not a simple process and the process will vary from one person to another depending on the level of determination of each individual. A Personal Revolution is about taking responsibility for our actions and the outcomes that we will reap.

The topic of change is monumental in the human condition; everyone talks about it; everyone says they want change. We all know that change is one of life's only constants and that it is inevitable, but when it actually happens it seems as if no one really wants it. And though we all undergo the same changes throughout our lives such as biological changes, the introduction of emerging technologies, changes in the parameters of our lives such as education, marriage and children, we all suffer because of it. So if we all know that change is inevitable and part of life then why do we make it difficult for ourselves? Well, because we become accustomed to circumstances and to the conditions in which we exist. It is in our human nature and part of our basic survival instincts to adapt to most situations including the difficult, undesirable ones. Everyone one has the potential to live a fulfilling authentic life; however achieving it requires that we face and surmount our deepest problems.

A Personal Revolution requires making a meaningful transformation in the way our minds work as the motivation for our behaviors begin in the mind. A successful human revolution requires us to put in certain amount of effort and to step out of our comforts zones. This type of transformation requires us to go through a profound internal transformation. This rarely happens spontaneously and immediately, though it does happen under extreme circumstances like natural disasters, a sudden death or a stroke of luck like winning the lottery, however most changes take place gradually and over extended periods of times. Nonetheless, a successful transformation is attainable and it is within anyone's grasp, the only thing that is required is that we look at the world differently.

Chapter 4

The Overbite Change Model

"You must be the change you wish to see in the world." Mahatma Gandhi

Anyone who's ever gone through the painful process of getting braces will easily relate to the process of achieving a lasting transformation. Often times we go through life apparently fine with whatever imperfections we may have until one day a single event or a series of events make us realize that we really dislike one particular thing about ourselves, in this case an overbite. From that moment on every time we look in the mirror we are bothered by the overbite because it makes us feel bad and because it affects various aspects of our life. We feel less attractive because of it; in addition to being affected physically we may also feel it affects us emotionally and psychologically. We may wonder to ourselves "If only I had pretty teeth maybe I would be more confident, maybe I would date more; maybe my life would be better". Finally the day comes when we decide to do something about it; we may come up with the idea to get braces to correct the overbite. Then go through the process of finding the right orthodontist, the painful process of figuring out how to pay for it.

Finally when the first set of steps is resolved we go through the painful ordeal of actually getting them installed. And once the braces are in place the overbite isn't corrected over night, is it? Of course not! It isn't corrected in a week or even a few months; sometimes the process may take years depending on the severity of the situation. All the while we learn new behaviors that help the overall outcome; we brush more diligently and may even change the types of food we eat. And though it may take a long time before we see the grand finally; that perfectly symmetrical smile; it does happen and the problem is resolved. This process applies to any significant change we make in our lives. Whether our fantasies about becoming more confident, dating more and having better lives become true or not all depend on what we make of our transformation, nonetheless the obstacle that we considered our setback; the overbite is fixed for good. Outlined below is the **Overbite Change Model**; let's see how it works.

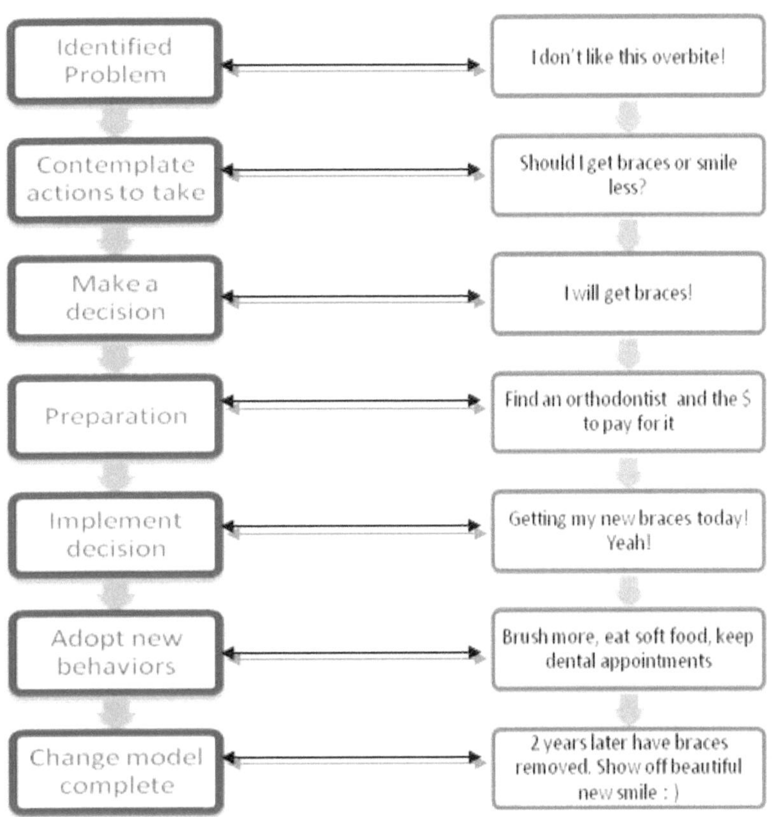

Now let's look at the seven steps of the **Overbite Change Model** individually as they apply in a personal revolution.

Step No. 1: Identify the Problem

The first step towards achieving a personal revolution begins with identify a particular problem, behavior or situation that you would like to change. In this step we need to figure the factors that are contributing to the paralysis of our careers. Now that you have read the wrap sheets for each of pigeonholes types you've probably identify with one or two types. You could have come up with any combination for instance: Yes Man with a side of Airhead or Bad Apple with a side of Slacker, whatever combination you came up with it will help you identify the characteristics and behaviors that you would like to improve or eliminate altogether. Here are a few questions to ask yourself which will help you get to the core factors that contribute your pigeonhole confinement.

- What pigeonhole type best describes me?
- Why do I identify with that particular pigeonhole type?
- What are the messages that I send out?
- What's the company and department culture?
- What is common theme?

Let's supposed you have come up with two scenarios:

In the first let's say you identify with the "Yes Man"; you might answer these questions like this:

"My boss is a tyrant and I am very afraid of losing my job so I always do what my boss asks me to do. Since I never stand up for myself my peers have lost respect for me. The company that I work for is notorious for firing people that speak up."

Clearly, the common theme is fear.

In the second let's say you identify with "The Bad Apple"; you might answer these questions like this:

"I really dislike my job and the role that I play in the organization. I don't care if my boss or my peers know it. Since the company is not loyal to me then I will not be loyal to the company."

Clearly, the common theme is disenchantment.

Now think of a time when you have played a different role; one in which you have been a successful, positive influence to your department and to the organization, either at another company or in the company where you are now. Ask yourself the same questions as above and then ask yourself:

- What was the theme then?
- What has changed since then?
- Have you changed positions?
- Has a new manager joined the team?
- Are you just tired of the same old thing?

Once you have answered these questions you may be able to analyze your situation and you may be able to pinpoint the factors that are contributing to your situation. Though you may come up with any combination of situations some common situations may be something like this.

> *"I was doing well in the company that I work until we got a new*
>
> *Manager who is a tyrant and now I cannot seem to do anything right."*

The problem in this scenario is not the new Manager, but rather there are two major factors that contribute to poor relationships.

- Lack of communication and/or a failure to communicate effectively what each others expectations are.
- Challenges with adapting to change.

"I used to like my job, but lately I'm bored and need new challenges"

The problem in this scenario is not lack of ambition or enthusiasm; those are just the symptoms of the real problem. The real problem is a displacement of talent which can happen when:

- We become too comfortable with the mundane.
- We fail to take risk and explore new challenges outside of our immediate responsibilities.

When you analyze your own situation you may noticed, that there are one or two factors that significantly stand out as major obstacles that keep you from becoming successful at your careers. These may be fear, comfort, reluctance to change, anger, etc. Once you have identified these factors you will be able to explore the possibilities of changing them.

Step No. 2: Contemplate Actions to Take

The second step towards achieving a human revolution involves dreaming up your possibilities. We operate in a world where practically every scenario imaginable is possible, we just have to find a vision and then make it happen. Part of contemplating a course of actions requires us to imagine our possibilities and our possibilities may be as simple or as extreme as we can imagine. For instance if you find yourself in a situation where people perceive you as a "Slacker" because you come to work 5 to 10 minutes late on a regular basis the possibilities can be as simple as leaving your home 15 minutes earlier. However, if you wanted to make an extreme change and wanted to be seen as "Go Getter" you might set your goals far higher than just a 15 minute adjustment at the beginning of your day. In addition to making it a habit of arriving to work on time, you might set the goal to become the best sales person in your department or you might volunteer for special cross departmental projects to learn different functions of the company. This would likely give you exposure to other departments and give you a specialty set of skills that would set you apart from your peers.

Whatever your possibilities, hopes and dreams may be remember to keep them BIG- I mean if we're going to dream they may dream big. See the way that dreams become come reality is very similar to the way that we hear things; the average person absorbs approximately 30% of what they hears, dreams are very similar to hearing in that the average person achieves portions of what they sets out to accomplish for that reason we should set high goals for ourselves.

Step No. 3: Make a Decision

Once you have mapped out all your possibilities and figured out which is the best suited for you, you'll have to make a decision. At this point you don't really have to figure out how you will get to the finish line you just have to know that you want a new situation in your life. This is similar to submitting an application to run in a marathon that may take place 6 months down the line. At that point you will only know for sure that you will participate in that marathon but you won't know all the details about your training, the weeks building up to the marathon or exactly what will happen the day of the run. There are only two things you need to do in this step, the rest will come in the consequent stages:

- Decide what changes you want in your life.
- Believe that you are capable of achieving them.

Step No. 4: Prepare

Once you have made a decision to change one particular aspect of your life you must prepare a plan of action and this is where the work really begins. In this step you begin to set realistic goals and road mapping a plan to get to your goals. One critical element in this step is to identify role models and anti-role models. Most of us know what a role model is; that is a person that you admire and find qualities in them that you would like to acquire for yourself. But you might be asking yourself “What is an anti-role model?” Well, this may be person that you may not particularly like moreover you do not admire them and their work ethic.

Role Model: When identifying your role model keep in mind that this can be anyone in your organization; it doesn’t have to be your direct supervisor or even an authority figure, though it might be. Consider everyone around you and see the various qualities that people have, sometimes we can find excellent role models among our peers, in people that we see with a strong work ethic or a particular talent that we would like to develop. Here are a few questions to keep in mind when identifying a role model.

- **“What does that guy have that I don’t have?”** If you carefully consider this question you will figure out that what a person that is more successful than you may have is something measurable and attainable. For instance if you admire a peer that was recently promoted from a similar position as yours you may find that that person may have more education or may have slight more experience that than you. But you should not consider that that person is somehow luckier than you or more talented because that would be placing your potential in the hands of fate and that is not what a human revolution is about. A human revolution is about seeking solutions to our problems and finding paths to our desired goals. To make myself perfectly clear I would like to share an example from my personal life. Some time ago I was in a romantic relationship with a gentleman that was the perfect 10. He was a young executive at a national television channel. You could say was a very eligible bachelor, young, handsome, great job and always upwardly mobile. From the outside looking in you would think this guy was on easy street, at least that's what I thought. We dated for about a year and then moved into together. Wow, what that an eye opening experience; he had made his life look so easy but the reality was that this was the hardest working individual I had ever met in my life. He was meticulously clean; he spent at least 2 hours at the gym every day. He would often as spend entire evenings working away at the computer to get his presentations perfect, more over he had fully control of his emotions and never showed a glimpse of anger. What I found out was that being a perfect 10 took a whole lot of effort and that it was a lifestyle not something that could be turned on and off.

- **"What do I admire about this person?"** Again after careful consideration you may find that you and the person that you admire already share similar traits, but they may have developed them to a level that you would like to attain for yourself. If this is the case, you're off to a good start.
- **"How do people perceive them?"** Remember the exercise in Chapter 1 about viewing your work place from the audience and movie director's perspective. Try it on your role model, this will help you get a better understanding of how people perceive than but more importantly it may give you a clue as to why they are perceived in that regard. What messages does this person send out? Then think to your self what actions or

behaviors do I have to adopt to send out the same types of messages. Please keep in mind that I am not asking you to become a clone of this person, only to identify the patterns in their behavior that you would like to develop for yourself.

Anti-Role Model- When setting our goals of transformation and planning our strategy we must also identify out weakness is, so the purpose of identifying an Anti-Role Model is very important. This will help us to see personality traits and patterns in anther person that we may deeply identify with ourselves and that would like to get rid of. For instance, let's say that you really dislike a person who is always whining and complaining but you do that yourself; looking at them well help you understand how people perceive you. Use your anti-role model to get out of your pigeonhole trap. Observe their actions and reactions and practice the exact opposite of what they do.

Once you have selected your Role Model and your Anti-Role Model create a list of short term and long term goals for you to achieve in your career. Short term goals would be changes that you can begin immediately. For instance, if you are viewed as a slacker and you have also identified a persons who is a slacker as an anti role model and that person arrives to work 5 to 10 minutes late on a regular basis. You can change that behavior in yourself tomorrow. Simply set your alarm clock 15 minutes earlier than usual.

On the other hand a long term behavior change which may require a period of 3 years to grow into. Let's say you are in an entry level position in a customer service center but hope to become the Manager or Director of that center. Well, you may identify that you do not have the education or experience needed for that position. A goal would be to pursue a higher education or to learn everything that there is to learn about that business. Trust me this may seem like unrealistic and unattainable goals but they are not. They are as simple as setting your alarm clock back 15 minutes; you just have to do it. Two years will go by in no time and you will find yourself in one of two scenarios.

- You will either still be contemplating “What does that guy have that I don’t have?”

OR

- You will be two years closer to your goal. Regardless of the career changes that may take place in the two years time, regardless of change in management or even if you change from one company to another, if you set a goal and begging to work towards it in two years time you will be that much closer to your human revolution.

Step No. 5: Implement Your Decision

Many of you may believe that this is the hardest step, but in reality you down all the hard work already. You’ve gone through the difficult process of saying “I’m not perfect”, “there are things about my life that I want to change”. Then you went through the process of thinking “Well, what else can I do, what are my alternatives” and then you found one. Implementing your decision is the day you actually go and have the braces installed. Once they are in the same as a decision being made they are pretty in place to stay. No reputable orthodontist will put in braces today and remove them tomorrow, the same with the implementing of your decision. Once you make it and implement it you have to stick to it.

Step No. 6: Adopt New Behaviors

Suppose you have decided to become the top sales person in your department. Well, it's an ambition but realistic decision. What happens next is that you have to as they say "Talk the Talk and Walk the Walk". Here is where your role models come in again. In order to learn the skills that you want to learn you have to have a general guide on how to get there. Again, I repeat you do not have to imitate every move of the person you have selected as a role model but you do have to learn the tricks of their traits. So, let's say you selected the top sales person in your department to shadow. Well, learn about the things they do outside of the general publics views to prepare to be the top sales person. This person may spend 30 minutes a day preparing by calling repeat customers or they may read books on human behavior, or simply have key words that they use that people love. These are the kind of things you'll want to adopt and customize to your own personality. You will soon learn that the factors that set this person aside and make them shine are nothing more than a good combination of habits; habits that you can acquire too. You may also find that those habits may not be easy to adapt to but over time you will gain a mastery of them. Steven Covey, Author of The 7 Habits of Highly Effective People says that "successful people are the people that do the things that nobody likes to do."

Step No. 7: Change Model Complete

In the final step of the change model you'll want acknowledge your success. So, let's say that a few weeks after you have made and implemented your decision, you look back to see the impact it has had in your life.

- You could be exactly where you expected to be when you first started.
- You can be somewhere along the lines of what you expected.
- You can even find yourself in on a completely different scenario than you were expecting.
- In the worst of cases you can be exactly as you were in the beginning with no change at all.

Part of completing the change model involves recognizing your growth and being able to gauge how successfully you've implemented your decision. If you did a good job and you are happy with your choices then you continue on your path towards success, but let's say for a minute that your efforts result in a complete and utter failure, you have to keep in mind that this is part of the changed model. As absurd as it may sound your failures will help you to grow and to become your best self. If one route fails you then you will know that the particular route is not for you and that can be counted as a success, because knowing what you've done wrong only gets you closer to what is correct for you.

Part III

Realization for Life

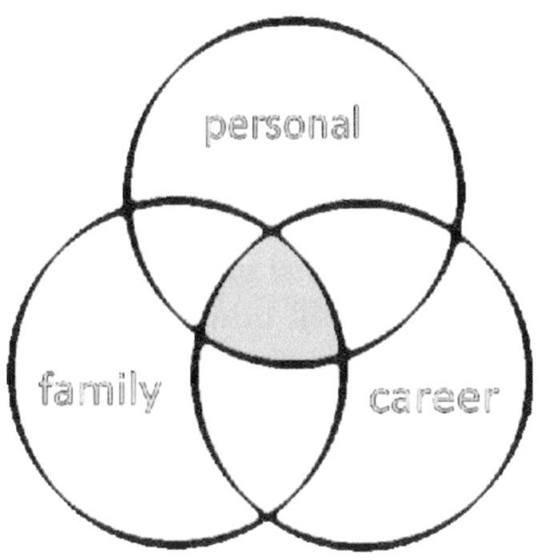

Chapter 5

Self Realization

> *"There are two ways to live: you can live as if nothing is a miracle; you can live as if everything is a miracle"*... Albert Einstein

First and foremost, now that you have completed the change model give yourself a pat on the back or a high five and celebrate your accomplishments; be truly grateful for what you have achieved thus far. It is also a time to self-reflect and to evaluate the changes that you have made in your life. However, self realization does not mean that now that you have become a great manager or a great director, you are completely realized. Some aspects of your life may be realized but self realization requires you to balance career, family and personal growth. If you focus exclusively on your career and completely abandon your family life or your personal growth then you will become a lopsided individual, which will bring about a whole new set of problems. So don't get too comfortable because the work of self-realization never ends. Self-realization is a life long trajectory from which we can easily be side tracked.

In a world of fluid change influenced by emerging technologies, new entrants to the market and the endless swaying of the political pendulum, we, too, must constantly change in order to stay in tune with rhythm of the world. The consequences when we grow into roles that give us greater responsibilities and higher levels of power we must continue to fine tune our knowledge in order to stay sharp. Sometimes a desire for more knowledge will come naturally as we achieve greater levels of success in our careers.

On the other hand, our success can also afford us many comforts which can become a dangerous trap. How often have you encountered the young executive that strives so hard to grow into a leadership position only to get lazy and stagnant once he/she achieves what he was striving for? This is a complete regression from a state of a personal revolution. How often you have you had a similar experience?

Let's do an exercise of self reflection: Think back 5 or 10 years ago when you actually dreamed of being in a position like the one you are in now. Now that you have achieved it you may feel trapped, once again. The Overbite Change Model discussed in chapter 4 can work for most situations; however the key to self-realization is not in achieving it but rather it is in constantly striving for it. When we continue to grow and to learn, we enter into a state that surpasses our simple financial and political ambition; surpassing these enters us into a pursuit of self-realization. Self realization can range from actions as simple as attempting to put oneself in another person's shoes to exploring a long lost personal interest. Whatever it is keep in mind that nothing is impossible and that nothing is wasted. Remember that Step No. 2 of the Overbite Change Model is to dream up all the possibilities that are out there for you.

Living in a state of self realization requires that we take responsibility to elevate ourselves in whatever position we may hold, we must also respect the positions and those around us as this will ultimately liberate you from the average to become a true leader.

Living in state of self realization also requires us to inspire others to grow and become their best selves. In chapter 2, I outlined the "before and after mindsets" of each of the pigeonholes you may have noticed pattern starting with an egotistical perspective in the before mind set which later becomes a positive pragmatic approach to helping one self and others. Helping others is the highest level of good you can do for yourself because it leads to strong alliances and gives you the opportunity to learn from others even if just to be able for one minute to get a different perspective outside of your own.

Once you reach your desired change or growth there is never a need to feel threatened when a new staff member wants to learn the skills that you have mastered. If someone comes to you for help, mentorship and advice it means that you've earned their respect and that you are the very best person at what you do. This should be as an opportunity for you to learn from each other and to move further in the direction of self-realization.

Ultimately, remember that the idea of Personal Revolution is about staying true to oneself and not allowing a label or higher status on the chain of command to shake your foundation of being the best you there is to be. The danger of losing our authenticity comes in when we become over zealous and greedy in our careers making status our number one priority. When this happens we end up trapped in new and bigger pigeonholes. Therefore we must maintain a balance to grow but to remain true to ourselves and our desires.

No two journeys are exactly alike; however the process of growth is exactly the same for all of us. First we must have an intention to grow and then take the steps needed to achieve our goals, and though no one can do it for us we can all learn from each other's experiences. I hope that my journey towards my own Personal Revolution will serve you as inspiration and guidance towards yours. In closing I would like to leave you with the one sentence from this book, which will lead you to success in your career and in all aspects of your life.

"The single most important thing that our readers can take away from this book is that no one will ever respect you unless you respect yourself first."

Respect yourself & others and thrive!

Work Cited

Bureau of Labor Statistics, < http://www.bls.gov/cps/>

Chopra, Deepak; (2003) The Spontaneous Fulfillment of Desire; Harnessing the Infinite Power of Coincidence.

Covey, Stephen; (1989), 7 Habits of Highly Effective People

Ford, Henry; < http://www.brainyquote.com/quotes/authors/h/enry_ford html>

Freud, Sigmund; (1855-1939) <http://thinkexist.com/quotation>

Gandhi, Mahatma; <http://thinkexist.com/quotation/you_must_ e _the_change_you_wish_to_see_in_the/14109.html>

Learning Café: < http://www.thelearning-cafe.com/html/ resource _links.html>

Reuters India, Reuters; from pigeons to multimedia player, April 17, 2008 <http://in.reuters.com/article/businessNews/idINIndia-33085020080417>

Samuelson, Paul A. <http://nobelprize.org/nobel_prizes/economics/laureates/1970/samuelson-bio.html>

Wikipedia: Albert Einstein; Theory of relativity <http://en.wikipedia.org/wiki/Theory_of_relativity>

www.ingramcontent.com/pod-product-compliance
Ingram Content Group UK Ltd.
Pitfield, Milton Keynes, MK11 3LW, UK
UKHW041926190726
13854UKWH00003B/1465

9 780557 323777